THE PEREGRINE FALCONS

THE PEREGRINE FALCONS
by Alice Schick
PICTURES BY PETER PARNALL

THE DIAL PRESS | NEW YORK

Library of Congress Cataloging in Publication Data
Schick, Alice. The peregrine falcons.
Bibliography: p. 1. Peregrine falcon—Juvenile literature.
[1. Peregrine falcon.   2. Falcons]   I. Parnall, Peter, ill.   II. Title
QL696.F34S34   *598.9'1*   *74-18599*
ISBN *0-8037-4917-6*   ISBN *0-8037-4972-4 lib. bdg.*

Printed in the United States of America | Second Printing 1976 for Alexander

FOREWORD

A decade ago few people thought the peregrine falcon had much chance of surviving in the wild, and even fewer felt that this aristocratic hunter, so much a creature of the open sky, could be bred successfully in captivity. At that time the wild falcons had already been eating prey contaminated with DDT for nearly twenty years, and they had totally disappeared as breeding birds from large parts of their range in North America and Europe. Only one man, a German falconer named Renz Waller, had ever been able to breed peregrines in confinement.

Since 1965 there has been a worldwide attempt by many concerned people to learn how to breed peregrines in captivity, so that young falcons can be returned one day to the wild places where their kind used to nest—on rocky crags overlooking our great rivers and along rugged, coastal palisades. By 1974, more than one hundred young peregrines had been hatched and raised in captivity, most of them in the preceding two years. Captive breeding has become an accomplished fact.

Meanwhile, man's use of DDT has greatly diminished in many parts of the world. In 1972 the federal government banned its use for almost all purposes in the United States. Now the peregrine has a chance to survive in nature.

Alice Schick has captured for her young readers the dramatic plight of the peregrine in the years since 1946, when DDT was first used on a large scale. In the chapters about Cadey and Heyoka—

a pair of captive peregrines—she effectively communicates the worry, excitement, and satisfaction all of us working with these great birds have shared as we learned how to propagate a wild creature in captivity.

Now that some of the peregrines have been released, we must wait to see whether they can survive to claim their eyries and breed in nature.

Dr. Tom J. Cade, *Professor of Ornithology*
The Peregrine Fund
Laboratory of Ornithology
Cornell University
Ithaca, New York

Contents

THE PEREGRINE FALCONS

CHAPTER ONE

A New Peregrine Pair

The bird swooped and turned in the air above the river. On long, slender but strong wings he climbed higher and higher into the sky, until he appeared to be no more than a dark speck hovering far above the four-hundred-foot cliff. Suddenly the bird began his descent. Keeping his wings folded close to his body, he shot downward at an incredible speed, in the motion that is called stooping.

He looked out of control. He would hit the water with a terrible impact. No living creature could hurtle a thousand feet out of the sky and survive.

But he did. Scarcely one hundred feet above the river, he braked with his wings and feet and landed lightly on a cliff ledge.

The bird rested there only a few seconds. Then he was off again, turning loops and figure eights above the river. Sometimes he disappeared, his slaty, blue-gray back impossible to see against the dark cliff. He was visible again when he turned, showing his whitish, speckled breast.

The bird continued his acrobatic display for twenty minutes. He seemed to be playing, inventing new stunts as he flew, showing off his amazing flying abilities. Twice more he climbed high above the cliff and rocketed down, stopping short and turning upward just before he hit the water.

Finally it was over, and the bird sat on one of the cliff ledges making drawn-out wailing noises at a larger bird on a nearby ledge.

The two birds were peregrine falcons. The beautiful, thrilling flight display was the male's way of courting the female. The male peregrine, about one-third smaller than the female, was called the tiercel, from a Latin word mean-

ing one third. The female was called simply the falcon.

This tiercel was no stranger to the cliff ledges. Every spring for the past eight years, since 1938, he and his mate had nested and raised their young on the towering cliffs called the Palisades on the west bank of the Hudson River.

The west bank of the river was wild and forested. Rocky ledges on the Palisades were ideal sites for peregrine nests. The east bank, which had no towering cliffs, was a good place for humans to settle. A number of towns dotted the Hudson's eastern shore.

Several people in the town opposite the tiercel's cliff liked to watch the peregrines through binoculars. They recognized the birds and welcomed them back to the nesting site year after year. One old man who watched the pair of peregrines even gave them names—Zeus and Hera, after the king and queen of the ancient Greek gods.

The names were fitting because peregrines were royal birds. They could fly faster than any other living creatures on earth, more than one hundred seventy-five miles an hour in a stoop. In medieval times, when birds of prey were often trained for hunting, peregrine falcons were reserved for noblemen. The men who trained the birds were called falconers, and the sport of hunting with birds of prey was called falconry. Peregrines were trained to hunt other birds and then return with the prey to their masters. Women of noble birth flew merlins, smaller cousins of the peregrines. Commoners had to be content with lesser birds of prey. In modern times, when the elaborate rules of medieval falconry had disappeared, falconers from every station in life wanted to own a peregrine more than any other hunting bird.

That March, in 1946, Hera had not returned to the nesting place on the Hudson. Zeus was performing his flight display for a new female perched on the ledge.

The female peregrine was a young bird, only two years old, with a few brownish juvenile feathers still visible in her almost-adult plumage. This would be her first breeding season, and if she accepted Zeus, he would be her first mate. Probably they would stay together until one of them died. Then the survivor would find a new mate, as Zeus was doing this spring.

The falcon was interested in Zeus. There was no doubt of that. Otherwise she could not have been lured to his cliff. But she was a cautious bird and had not quite made up her mind. The tiercel would have to convince her.

Zeus continued calling to the falcon, coaxing her to join him at the nesting ledge. The female did not move. She watched the tiercel with interest but was silent.

She was a beautiful bird, big even for a female peregrine.

She was twenty-one inches long from the top of her head to the tip of her square tail. Zeus, the tiercel, was merely fifteen inches in length, about average size for a male bird.

Trying a new tactic to win the falcon, Zeus flew to a ledge near the top of the cliff. This perch was a lookout ledge. It jutted out far into the river. From there the tiercel could keep a sharp eye on both river banks for more than a mile around.

Zeus scanned the sky. Then with a wailing cry to make sure the falcon was watching, he took off. He flew north and east, over the middle of the river. He did not seem to hurry, and to human eyes there seemed to be no special purpose to the flight.

But peregrine eyesight is better than human eyesight—about seven times better—and Zeus had spotted his prey. Gradually Zeus gained speed and altitude. By the time the blue jay noticed him, the tiercel was directly over his head, perhaps two hundred feet up.

The blue jay, panicked now, flew as fast as he could, trying to reach the trees on the east bank of the river. It was too late. The tiercel dropped out of the sky, his strong yellow feet extended. His three front toes were curled into a fist. His back toe with its sharp claw was pointed downward. With this talon, Zeus slammed into his prey.

The blue jay had no time to realize what had happened and no time to suffer. He died instantly. His body began to fall toward the river.

With lightning speed Zeus shot beneath the falling jay. Turning upward, he caught the bird in his talons only a few feet above the water. The tiercel righted himself and, holding his prey in one foot, headed back toward the west bank and the falcon.

It was all part of nature's cycle, where sooner or later every creature becomes food for another species. When the peregrine died, there would be something to eat his remains. Nothing would be wasted.

While Zeus lived, he would continue to hunt, killing his prey quickly and cleanly. And in a way, like all predators, he would be performing a service for the species he hunted.

Zeus wasn't always successful when he hunted. Sometimes he went after a bird and missed. A strong, healthy, smart blue jay had a good chance to get away. Most of Zeus' catches were the weaker ones—the birds who were old or sick or stupid. That way, only the strongest blue jays lived to breed. If they all had survived, there would soon have been too many blue jays competing for the same food and space, and all of them would have suffered.

Zeus reached the cliff with his prey. The tiercel flew past

the ledge where the falcon waited. He dipped toward her and called, using his wailing cry. Then he moved out toward the middle of the river. He circled back in the direction of the cliff, passing the falcon and calling again.

This time she responded to his cries. The falcon took flight, swooping gracefully in front of the cliff. Now that both birds were airborne, it was easy to see just how much larger the female was. From the tip of one wing to the tip of the other, she measured just over three feet.

The falcon called the wailing cry to the tiercel, who circled above her, the dead blue jay still in his foot. Suddenly Zeus released the prey. The falcon stooped at it, using the same folded-wings dive the tiercel had used in hunting.

She caught the prey easily and returned with it to one of the cliff ledges. She took the jay's neck in her beak, and with the notch that is called the falcon's tooth, she cut the bird's spinal cord. If the jay had not already been dead, this would have killed it.

The falcon held down her prey with one foot. Using the strong, hooked tip of her beak, she began to pull off its feathers, an action that is called pluming. When a part of the jay was cleaned, she began to feed.

While she plumed the blue jay, Zeus watched her from the air. When she started to eat, he landed on the ledge where she was feeding. He called to her, this time in a softer voice, a cry that sounded like *eechup*. She returned the call, then continued eating. The tiercel watched intently as the falcon ate the blue jay.

The falcon would be Zeus' new mate. She had accepted his gift of food. That meant she would now accept him.

Again there would be peregrine falcons nesting on the cliff above the Hudson. The old man who had named the tiercel decided to call the new falcon Artemis, after the Greek hunting goddess.

CHAPTER TWO

The Nesting Ledge

The day was ending. The sun sank in the western sky behind the woods that capped the Palisades. The gray cliffs with the peregrines' nesting, feeding, and lookout ledges were in deep shadow, making it nearly impossible to see the birds from across the river.

The two peregrines had finished eating. They were content to remain quietly together on the ledge. Sometimes they seemed almost as if they were talking. Zeus would chirp softly and Artemis would answer *eechup*.

There would be no more aerial acrobatics that day. The peregrine falcons did not fly at night. Instead, Zeus began to preen, using his beak to clean and rearrange his feathers. With great care he drew each feather through his beak, as if he were zipping it up. Preening was necessary, for if his feathers became dirty and rumpled, he would not be able to fly, at least not well enough to hunt.

Artemis also preened carefully. She shook her body, ruffling her feathers, which made her look as if she had been caught in a strong wind. This helped her to separate the feathers so she could attend to each one in turn.

After a while the two birds began to preen each other. Gently using the tip of her hooked beak, Artemis nibbled at the feathers on the tiercel's breast. When she was finished, she bent her head forward and chirped, inviting Zeus to preen her neck. He accepted the invitation.

The birds' mutual preening served a practical purpose. One bird could not clean its own face or the back of its head. The other peregrine was helpful in keeping hard-to-reach feathers clean and in good condition.

But mutual preening had another purpose too. It was part

of the birds' courtship. Preening helped to establish the bond between Zeus and Artemis, to strengthen their ties to one another, and make sure they would stay together for many years.

The peregrines would preen each other many times in the next few weeks. Their fierce, strong beaks, designed and skillfully used for tearing meat, could also be used with great delicacy to express affection, through preening and billing. Zeus and Artemis would often touch beaks, nibbling and playing.

As darkness fell, the two peregrines moved to their night perch. This was a long ledge so narrow that the birds had to stand sideways on it. Although to human eyes it looked uncomfortable, the ledge had one feature that made it a perfect sleeping place for the falcons—an overhang. On their narrow night ledge the birds were protected from biting wind and icy rain. They could sleep comfortably through any storm.

The next day Zeus and Artemis awoke at dawn when the first rays of sunlight from the east struck the cliff. They spent the next two hours on the ledge, preening and billing and just looking around. By eight o'clock both birds were airborne. They seemed to be aware of one another, but they did

not really fly together. Each seemed to be flying for its own enjoyment.

To the humans watching from the east bank of the river, the peregrines looked as if they were playing. A purely practical person might have said the birds were exercising, keeping in shape for hunting. But no matter what made Zeus and Artemis fly, it was easy to see that they enjoyed it.

Artemis flew out over the river, then back to the cliff in a straight line. She rested for a few seconds on the lookout ledge, then took off again. Her second flight was longer and included graceful dips and turns in the air. Afterward, she returned to the cliff again.

When she launched herself for the third time, her long wings carried her out over the river and high above the cliff. From there she made a series of breathtaking dives, each time stopping in mid-air and turning upward again.

Although she was agile and quick, Artemis could not maneuver quite as well as the tiercel. Her turns were slightly wider and slower. This was partly because Zeus was an older, more experienced bird, but the main reason was the difference in size. The smaller male peregrine needed less room for turning and could change direction faster.

The larger falcon was more capable than the tiercel of protecting eggs and young birds in the nest. For several weeks, until the eggs were laid and hatched and the young birds were three weeks old, the falcon would spend most of her time at the nest. The tiercel would hunt for everyone. Later, when the growing young needed less protection and more food, the falcon would hunt again. Her larger size and greater strength would permit her to take larger prey than the tiercel would attack.

When Artemis gathered speed and headed purposefully out over the river, Zeus watched from one of the ledges. He knew that his mate was hunting, and it was time for him to hunt also. It took him only a few seconds to spot a suitable target, a small bird flying close to the cliff top, near the line of trees.

There was not enough time for the tiercel to climb high in the sky and strike the sparrow from above. The bird would see him and fly into the woods on the cliff top, where the peregrine would not follow. But Zeus did not need to strike from above. He launched himself toward the sparrow. When he was even with his prey and just below it, he rolled quickly in mid-air and caught the little bird in his foot.

Zeus returned with the bird to the feeding ledge, killed and plumed it quickly, and began to eat. The sparrow was small, smaller than his usual prey, but he would not have to share it with Artemis. Zeus would hunt again in the afternoon.

The falcon's hunting was also successful. Her kill, made far up the river, was a large flicker, a kind of woodpecker. The bird would make a full meal, and the falcon might not eat again until tomorrow.

When they had eaten, the peregrines rested and preened. Artemis seemed sleepy, as if she wanted a nap, but Zeus hopped around uneasily. He made several short display flights over the river. Each time he left, he acted anxious to return. When he landed, he called to the falcon again and again.

More and more often Zeus landed on the nesting ledge. From there he made his wailing cry at Artemis, as if he were trying to show her how perfect a nesting place it was.

It was a good ledge for the eyrie, as the peregrines' nest is called. The tiercel and his old mate had used it for several years and each year had raised one or more young there. But now Zeus could do no more than show it to Artemis. The falcon would have to make the final selection.

After much calling by Zeus, Artemis finally flew over to the ledge. The tiercel scratched about furiously in the gravel,

making sure his new mate did not overlook the ledge's best features.

Zeus fussed and called loudly all around the falcon. Artemis answered with long, loud *eechup* cries. After a few minutes the falcon flew to a small ledge close by. Zeus followed and eventually coaxed her to another ledge suitable for a nest.

Face to face, the two birds called and bowed to each other. First the tiercel, then the falcon scraped at the gravel on the ledge. They scraped together for a while and then stopped to bill one another.

Zeus showed his mate a number of different nesting sites, making scrapes on each ledge. The peregrines billed and called at each site, but Artemis acted as if she were not yet ready to make a final selection.

The following day, on one of the cliff ledges, the tiercel mounted the falcon, and the birds mated for the first time. They would mate several times a day until Artemis began to lay eggs.

Just as if she had nested many times before, Artemis grew serious about choosing a nesting ledge as soon as the mating began. When Zeus hunted, she flew from ledge to ledge, inspecting the scrapes the tiercel had made earlier as if she were seeing each one for the first time.

She hunted less, preferring to let Zeus bring her food and plume it for her. She had more important concerns now. On the sixth day after the peregrines first mated, Artemis chose her nesting ledge—the same broad ledge that the tiercel had first shown her.

CHAPTER THREE

In the Eyrie

Once she had chosen a ledge, Artemis began to prepare the nest. There was no time to waste, for she would soon be ready to lay the eggs. She scratched with determination at the small scrape Zeus had made in the gravel until she had hollowed out a shallow depression that just fit her body. In a little while she was finished, and she rested in the hollow she had made, trying it out for size. Whenever the tiercel was not hunting, he returned to the nesting ledge to watch his mate, call to her, and scratch about.

The depression in the gravel was all the nest the peregrine needed. It would be enough to keep the eggs from rolling off the ledge.

That whole day Artemis left the nesting ledge only once, to feed briefly on a bird Zeus had caught. She ate quickly and returned to the eyrie to lay the first egg. It was smaller and much rounder than a chicken's egg. It was also much more colorful, a beautiful creamy, warm red tone, splashed with darker red-brown spots.

Two days later, during the second week in April, Artemis laid a second egg, and two days after that, a third. Each tiny unborn peregrine, called an embryo, had started to develop when it was still inside the falcon's body, before its egg was laid. After the first and second eggs were laid, the embryos inside them stopped growing for a while. The parent birds were not yet ready to sit on, or incubate, the eggs. They would wait until most of the eggs were laid. When incubation began, all the embryos would start growing again. That way, all the baby peregrines would be ready to hatch at about the same time.

With the laying of the third egg, the falcon began to incubate, using her body to keep the eggs warm. The bird's feathers were designed to insulate, to keep body heat from escaping. In order to warm her eggs, the falcon had two brood spots on the under part of her body, one on each side of her breast. These were patches of bare skin with many blood vessels near the surface. When Artemis parted her feathers in just the right way, the brood spots lay close against the eggs. If the eggs had been allowed to grow cold after incubation began, the embryos growing inside would have died.

Regularly, Artemis turned the eggs in the gravel nest, making sure that each egg stayed warm all over so that each baby developed properly. No one taught her to do this. Caring for her eggs was as natural to Artemis as her need to hunt.

The humans who watched the peregrines could tell from the birds' behavior that there were eggs in the nest, but they couldn't see the eggs themselves. Four was the usual clutch size—the number of eggs—in a peregrine falcon eyrie. But there might be as many as five eggs or as few as two. The peregrine watchers would not know there were three eggs until the babies hatched, in about thirty-two days.

For most of each day, Artemis sat on the nest, incubating the eggs. Zeus hunted for both birds. When he caught some-

thing for his mate, she left the eyrie to catch the prey in mid-air.

When the falcon first laid the eggs, the tiercel sometimes offered to take over the job of incubation. Stooping in front of the nesting ledge, he called to his mate, tempting her to fly. Once, he landed on the ledge, bowed to Artemis, stretched out his neck and called, begging for a chance to sit on the eggs. But Artemis scolded him with a loud cry and chased him away.

The tiercel was not accustomed to such behavior. His first mate, Hera, had always allowed him much time with their eggs. It had been her habit to fly at least once, but usually twice a day. Sometimes she had hunted. Other times she had merely played. Hera had acted as if flying were too great a joy to give up. She seemed to know that Zeus would care for the eggs while she was away from the eyrie.

Artemis was different. She seemed reluctant to leave her eggs for any reason. Occasionally, she allowed Zeus to cover the eggs for an hour or more while she hunted for herself. But usually the tiercel incubated only while his mate was on the feeding ledge with prey he had caught for her. Artemis ate quickly, returning to the eggs to chase her mate away.

As the days passed, Artemis grew more and more jealous of the eggs. She seemed to hate leaving them even for a few minutes. She no longer hunted for herself at all, and she regularly finished the food Zeus brought in ten minutes or less.

Instead of incubating the eggs, Zeus became a fierce protector of the nest. In early spring, huge flocks of migrating birds used the Hudson River flyway. Each day hundreds of birds passed the cliff eyrie on their way north to their own nesting places. Any bird that ventured too close to the ledge where Artemis sat on the three spotted eggs suddenly found itself Zeus' target. The tiercel stooped repeatedly at the hapless bird, scaring it so badly that it would never again venture near the cliff.

Zeus rarely struck any of the birds he frightened. He killed only for food or if something deliberately threatened him, his mate, or his young.

During the month of quiet incubation Artemis began her molt. The peregrines, like all birds, molted every year. Old feathers became worn out and had to be replaced. Unlike birds of some species, Artemis did not lose all her feathers at the same time. Then she would have been unable to fly while she waited for new feathers to grow. Instead, she lost only a few feathers at a time. She could not fly as well as usual with feathers missing, but she could fly well enough to catch the food Zeus brought her. Artemis would have most of her new feathers by the time she had to find food for her growing chicks.

The tiercel's molt began between two and three weeks after the falcon's. Zeus' molt would follow a different pattern. He would lose only a feather or two at a time. Throughout the molt he would fly as well as ever, but because it went so slowly, it would be autumn before his new set of feathers was complete.

For a month, Artemis cared for her eggs while Zeus fed and protected her. Two days before the chicks were ready to hatch, they started to make chirping noises inside the eggs. The chirping grew stronger and more insistent as the time for hatching drew near. Artemis could not ignore the sounds. She cocked her head curiously, and somehow she knew the noises came from her babies. She answered with a gentle clucking she would continue to use while the chicks were young.

And then, on a bright May morning, the eggs were ready to hatch. Now the falcon refused to leave the nest at all. She was not interested in the food brought by the tiercel. He called to her, but she ignored him. Artemis would not leave the nest until the chicks broke out of the eggs.

The hatching took a long time. Breaking through the hard eggshell was a difficult job for a tiny bird. An about-to-be-born peregrine had only one tool, a patch of hard, scratchy material on the tip of its beak. This "egg tooth" would disappear in a few weeks, but now the first young peregrine relied on it to peck and saw its way out of the egg.

Finally, by late afternoon, one baby split its eggshell in two and crawled out. The newborn eyass, as a young peregrine is called, looked nothing like its parents. Artemis eyed her first baby with interest. The little bird, still wet from the egg, looked almost naked. Really, though, it was covered with creamy white down that would be soft and beautiful just as soon as it dried. The bird's eyes were tightly shut, not yet developed enough to face the light of day. Soon, the chick would be able to open its eyes, but it would not open them wide. For several days the little peregrine's eyes would be weak, able to distinguish only vague shapes and light from dark. Its head looked far too big for its body, and the pencil-thin neck could not support it for more than a second.

The eyass was exhausted from its struggle to break out of the egg and too weak to do anything but push feebly under Artemis for warmth. It looked as if it hadn't really been ready to leave the egg.

But the baby had to hatch when it did. It had used up the food supply inside the egg and now needed its parents to provide food so it could live and grow.

By the following evening all three eggs had hatched. Artemis had carefully cleaned out the nest by dropping the pieces of eggshell over the edge of the eyrie. Now she and Zeus would be busier than ever, taking care of their demanding brood.

CHAPTER FOUR

Three Young Peregrines

The falcon remained close to the eyrie. The eyasses were cold-blooded for the first few days of life; their body temperature depended on the temperature of their environment, and they could freeze to death on a chilly day. So the falcon kept them warm and secure under her body.

Though the eyasses were still tiny and nearly blind, their

appetites were enormous. They chirped and fussed as best they could, constantly reminding their parents that they were hungry.

Not that the adult birds needed reminding. They took the business of raising their young very seriously. They seemed to know that the eyasses needed constant attention.

Zeus had no time to relax. He now had four other birds dependent on him for food. He played less and hunted more. When he returned to the cliff with prey, he called to Artemis, and she came at once. She caught the prey as he dropped it and took it back to the eyrie.

While Zeus was responsible for hunting, Artemis fed the young chicks. She tore off tiny strips of meat and held them in her beak. Then she clucked to her babies, coaxing them to take the food from her.

The eyasses grew rapidly. By the time they were ten days old, their eyes had opened wide, and their soft white down was turning coarse. The second coat of down, dingy white and stubby, would protect the chicks until their first real feathers grew. The three eyasses were much bigger now, and they were stronger, too. Sometimes they sat up on the ledge, moving their heads and looking all around them with interest.

The young peregrines sat in a most undignified fashion, with their weak legs stuck out straight in front of them. At

this age, their feet were not yellow like those of their parents, but very pale, with a hint of blue. The chicks' bodies gave no hint of the strong, streamlined shapes they would become. The babies were front-heavy, their little stomachs bulging from the enormous meals they ate every day. It looked almost as if somehow Zeus and Artemis had hatched the wrong eggs. It seemed impossible that the eyasses would ever look like peregrines.

The next week, the little falcons were bigger and stronger. Although they still spent many hours a day sprawled on their stomachs, they could scramble awkwardly all over the nesting ledge. Miraculously, they managed to keep away from the edge. Without being taught, they seemed to fear the long drop to the river. In a few weeks, the eyasses would have to conquer their inborn fear of the edge. If they didn't, they would never learn to fly. But for now that fear saved their lives.

The eyasses had discovered the full range of their voices. They could make a variety of sounds and seemed to enjoy trying them out. They called loudly for their food and screamed frantically when they saw Zeus approach the eyrie with prey.

When food came, they scrambled and fought to reach it first. No longer did they need Artemis to tear off strips of meat for them. They could peck and tear at a bird by them-selves. Of course, they were clumsy and needed some help from their parents. The young birds still knew nothing of pluming. Often Zeus and Artemis brought their babies the remains of a kill when they were finished eating. That way, the prey was cleaned, and the eyasses could easily get at the meat.

When the young peregrines were three weeks old, Artemis' molt stopped, and she began to hunt again. She would com-plete her molt when the young were independent. The babies were growing every day, gaining the strength they would soon need for flying. They no longer needed their mother's constant protection. Besides, their demands for food had in-creased to the point where Zeus could not meet them alone. From now on both parents would hunt for their young, until the young could hunt for themselves.

The two adult peregrines were almost always in the air, stooping at prey to feed their chicks. Zeus caught blue jays and flickers and swallows and fat racing pigeons. Artemis sometimes took larger prey—shorebirds nesting on the Hud-son's banks, green herons, once even a duck.

The eyasses were almost ready to fly. They were beginning to get their first real feathers, the buff-and-brown-streaked plumage of juvenile peregrines. The first feathers appeared on their wings and tails. These were the feathers they would need for flying and were the longest and strongest on their bodies. The young birds looked strange with their new feathers pushing through the coarse down.

The chicks had grown very large after four weeks, and for the first time a peregrine watcher could tell that there were two falcons and one smaller tiercel. The male was fully grown first. The falcons, with more growing to do, reached full size a few days later.

The young tiercel was a dark-colored bird. The brown of his juvenile plumage was rich and almost shiny. His breast was so heavily streaked that it looked as brown as his back, with only a few light spots. One of his sisters was similarly colored, with just a bit more white on her breast. The other young falcon was much lighter, a soft golden brown on the back, with a lightly streaked yellowish breast.

Except for their coloring, the three young peregrines now looked like adult birds. Their wings were the long, narrow wings of their parents. Like the adults, they weighed surprisingly little in comparison to their size: The tiercel weighed about one and a half pounds, and the larger falcons, two pounds. Very little of their weight was bone. As the chicks grew, air spaces had formed inside their bones, making their skeletons very light. Their bodies had converted their baby-fat fronts into powerful breast muscles that anchored their wings and would make them superb flyers.

Physically, the eyasses were ready to fly. Psychologically, flying was another matter entirely. The three chicks seemed not at all convinced that leaving the eyrie was a good idea.

Their parents regarded matters differently. Zeus and Artemis seemed to know that the eyasses must soon be on their own. The parents' behavior helped the young birds develop their natural talents for flying and hunting. Instead of landing on the nesting ledge with prey for the young birds, a parent would fly close to the ledge, turn sideways, and drop the prey close to the brink of the ledge without stopping. This helped to train the young but also helped to protect the parents. In their eagerness to feed, the three grown babies could easily have injured an adult bringing them a meal. The chicks would plume the prey awkwardly, squabbling among themselves all the while.

After a few days of receiving food this new way, the eyasses learned to crowd together at the edge of the eyrie when a parent approached with prey. They pushed each other about and called loudly.

Zeus and Artemis began to tease their young with the prey. They would fly back and forth in front of the nesting ledge, dipping and calling with the wailing cry, trying to make the chicks fly. Each day, the teasing continued a little longer before the parents gave in and dropped a dead bird on the ledge. Each day, the eyasses grew more frantic in their struggle to get at the food.

Finally, one day just before the eyasses were five weeks old, Artemis caught and killed a large woodpecker. She glided past the eyrie with the bird in her talons and called to her young. As usual, the eyasses jumped and squawked and pushed. Then suddenly the young tiercel stepped off the ledge and was airborne for the first time. Maybe he sensed that his mother would refuse to drop the prey on the ledge. Maybe he was tired of being pushed away from his food by his larger sisters. Whatever the reason, he was in the air.

For a second the young tiercel seemed panicked and unsteady. But only for a second. He was a born flyer, and his inborn knowledge guided him now as he hung there three hundred feet above the Hudson River. Somehow he knew when to flap his wings, when to spread his tail feathers, and when to do a thousand other things he had never done before.

Artemis climbed rapidly, still holding the woodpecker. She called to her son to keep his attention. When she was directly above him, she released the prey.

Without a moment's hesitation, the young tiercel folded

his wings and dived at the falling bird. Whether from in-
stinct or from watching his parents, he understood what he
was supposed to do. But his inexperience showed. He mis-
calculated and plunged right past his prey. His talons
clutched only air.

Fortunately, his mother was watching. Deftly, Artemis re-
covered the woodpecker a few seconds before it hit the water.
She climbed above the cliff to repeat the lesson.

The second time, the young tiercel caught the bird. He
carried it off to a nearby ledge, where he began to plume it
in his clumsy, unpracticed fashion. He obviously had no in-
tention of taking it to the eyrie, where his sisters would
roughly demand their share. Instead, for the first time in his
life, he ate slowly and peacefully. A human might have said
the young tiercel seemed proud of himself.

The two young falcons remained on the nesting ledge.
They watched their brother's first flight intently and saw his
reward. The golden brown, light-colored falcon seemed to
make the connection between flight and food. She launched
herself as soon as Zeus appeared in the distance, flying toward the eyrie with prey.

The third chick, the darker female, knew what she had
to do but seemed frightened. Several times she spread her
wings and lifted herself a few inches off the ledge. But she

was careful to keep the ledge beneath her. There was no reason why she couldn't fly as well as the others. She was just more cautious than her sister or her brother. She needed more coaxing before she tried anything new.

The young tiercel and the light-colored falcon had been flying for two days before the second young falcon finally took to the air. She quickly made up for lost time and by the following day could fly as well as the others.

Five weeks after hatching, the young peregrines had their juvenile plumage and had left the nest to fly. Even so, they were not yet ready to fend for themselves. Much flying practice lay ahead. And the young birds still had to master the art of hunting.

The babies loved to fly. Often the three young birds and their parents were in the air at the same time. The peregrines stooped at each other playfully.

Without realizing it, Zeus and Artemis were training their children to be independent hunters. The young birds were exercising their muscles and practicing essential peregrine skills.

For a month after the young birds first flew, the parents continued to feed them. However, Zeus and Artemis did not permit their young to sit idly on the ledge waiting for a meal. They required them to catch their prey in mid-air.

Often the parents worked together. Artemis might kill a bird and drop it to a young falcon flying below her. Zeus would fly lower still, prepared to recover the prey if his daughter missed it.

When Zeus and Artemis were off hunting, the young peregrines started to try hunting on their own. At first they could catch nothing, and they would have starved if their parents had not continued to drop dead prey for them.

But gradually the birds' skills improved. They grew stronger and surer. Within a few weeks, the three young peregrines had caught and killed their own prey. They looked like expert hunters, using their feet to strike and their beaks to kill. They no longer needed their parents. Zeus and Artemis had successfully raised their young to independence.

CHAPTER FIVE

The Peregrines in Winter

Summer was ending on the Palisades by the time the three young peregrines became independent hunters. Leaves on the trees along the Hudson's banks turned orange and gold and red. There was a new crispness in the air telling all living creatures that winter was coming.

The southward migrations began. Most birds were finished with the difficult job of rearing their broods. The young were able to fly and find their own food. It was time to leave the northern breeding grounds and head for warmer climates.

Again, as it had been in spring, the Hudson River was a great flyway. Now in the fall all traffic flowed in the opposite direction—one way going south.

Some birds who nested in the far north migrated only as far as the Hudson Valley in wintertime. To them, that was south. And some birds did not migrate at all. The clever, resourceful blue jays, for example, had no trouble finding food and shelter in winter. There would be plenty of birdlife along the Palisades even when the snow and icy winds came, plenty of food for peregrine falcons.

The name peregrine comes from the Latin word for "wanderer," and many peregrines did migrate. The Arctic peregrines who nested in Alaska and northern Canada spent their winters along the southern coast of the United States. Some went as far as South America. But the Hudson River peregrines were not great wanderers. Zeus and Artemis would remain on the Palisades almost all year. Except for a couple of mid-winter months spent on the Atlantic coast, they would stay near their nesting cliff until the following spring.

Their responsibilities toward their young finished, the tiercel and the falcon were birds of leisure again. Hunting was easy during the migrations. The peregrines had time to fly for no special purpose, to play.

Fall gave way to winter and still the three young peregrines remained near the cliffs, not too many miles from where they were born.

To the young tiercel the Palisades meant home. When spring came he, like most male peregrines, would search the riverside near his birthplace until he found a cliff he could claim as his own. He would not find a mate and breed until the following spring, when he was two years old. But he might stake out a territory and defend it at the age of one.

Typically, the two young falcons did not feel the same ties to the Palisades as their brother. When they reached breeding age at two, they might find mates along the Hudson, but they might also choose some other area of the northeast to look for mates.

This first winter, though, the dark-colored young female, the cautious one, seemed perfectly content to remain near her birthplace. She displayed little urge to explore.

Her sister, the big, light-colored falcon, was different. Always the adventurous one, she had ranged farther from her birthplace than her nestmates. From their first hunts she had gone after larger, stronger prey than her brother or sister.

The peregrine watchers on the east bank of the river noticed the different personalities of the young birds. The large, golden falcon with the brave heart captured the admiration of the old man who had named Zeus and Artemis. He called the adventurous falcon Nike, after the winged Greek goddess of victory.

In November the first snow fell along the Hudson. The snow seemed to be a signal to Nike, telling her it was time to leave. She did not migrate like the Arctic peregrines, who headed for warm weather. Instead she flew south for only thirty miles until, on the east bank of the river, the city of New York lay before her.

The habitat was man-made, designed for people, not peregrines. Still, something about the city drew the young falcon and held her. The vertical stone and brick walls of skyscrapers were not unlike the cliffs she knew. Tall buildings had window ledges and overhangs where a peregrine could find shelter.

Nike made her winter home on a window ledge of a thirty-story building overlooking the river. From her lookout post atop a stone lion that adorned the building, she could see the George Washington Bridge spanning the Hudson.

The huge bridge provided shelter for many birds. Tucked under the roadway, high above the water, was a starling roost. There, thousands of the noisy blackbirds lived. When the flock took to the air, it was a simple matter for the young falcon to capture a meal.

With the starlings so close, Nike rarely looked for other prey. Every now and then she went after a racing pigeon, enjoying the challenge of capturing a fast-flying bird. The racing pigeons had been trained by human owners to fly straight and fast, not to stop and take cover when pursued. The peregrine falcon quickly learned to take advantage of the pigeons' habits.

After two unsuccessful attempts, Nike stopped trying to hunt ordinary city street pigeons. From a peregrine's point of view, street pigeons had the bad habit of taking cover when threatened. Often they refused to fly at all. They walked around the gutters, pecking at breadcrusts, completely absorbed in their own search for food. The pigeons sometimes didn't even look up when a peregrine flew overhead. They seemed to realize that peregrines rarely attack nonflying prey. The peregrine's long wings, designed for maneuvering in open space, were inefficient in the canyons of the city streets.

Nike was one of fifteen peregrines who spent the winter

on New York skyscrapers. Like her, most of the birds were young females who had not yet found mates. A few, like Nike, came from eyries along the Hudson River. Others had been hatched farther north, on New England cliffs in Massachusetts, Vermont, New Hampshire, or Maine.

Only one mated pair of peregrines spent that winter in New York. For them, a city building was home, just as the cliff on the Palisades was home for Zeus and Artemis. The city peregrines had nested on a ledge of the building. Their eggs hatched and their eyasses were thriving when someone deliberately killed the young birds.

During a ten-year period, from 1943 to 1953, this pair of city peregrines successfully hatched four clutches of eggs on two different skyscrapers. Each time, the eyasses were either killed or taken to be trained for sport hunting by falconers.

The young peregrines were killed before they were old enough to fly. There were many New Yorkers who would have killed the adult peregrines too if they had been able to catch them. Only their ability to fly kept Nike and the other wintering birds safe.

Few people understood the part peregrine falcons and other predators played in nature's cycle. To pigeon fanciers, peregrine falcons were a menace. To lovers of songbirds, peregrine falcons were vicious killers. Some people even be-

49

lieved peregrines were dangerous to humans. New York newspapers printed reports of supposed peregrine falcon attacks on people as well as sensational accounts of pigeon "murders" by peregrines.

Not all city-dwellers disliked the birds. In fact, while New Yorkers tried to get rid of their peregrines, the people of Montreal, Canada, did everything they could to make their special falcon feel at home.

In the spring of 1937 a yearling female peregrine took up residence on a ledge of Montreal's Sun-Life Insurance Building. The next spring, ready to breed, she returned with a mate.

The peregrines courted and mated on the Montreal skyscraper. The falcon laid her eggs in a drainpipe. Unfortunately, the eggs rolled away, and the birds could not incubate them. In spite of the nesting failure, the peregrines returned the next year and tried again. And again, the lack of a proper nesting ledge spoiled their chances.

Then someone in the building had an idea. A special man-made nesting ledge was designed for the peregrines. The square nesting tray was filled with gravel and hung from a twentieth-story window.

The birds accepted the strange ledge and, for the first time, hatched young. The baby peregrines grew up only a few feet and a window away from the desks of dozens of office workers.

Year after year, the Sun-Life falcon returned to the Montreal skyscraper. When she lost her first mate, she returned with another tiercel, and later, a third. In the years between 1940 and 1952 she successfully raised more than twenty young.

The Sun-Life falcon proved that peregrines could thrive closer to man than anyone had ever dreamed. If they were protected and appreciated instead of persecuted, peregrine falcons could live right in the heart of a bustling, modern city.

CHAPTER SIX

The Peregrines Disappear

As winter ended, the peregrines' annual breeding cycle began once again. On their rocky cliff high above the Hudson River, Zeus the tiercel and Artemis the falcon prepared for a new clutch.

The spring of 1947 was another good one for the Palisades peregrines. Zeus and Artemis hatched four young and raised two. Even though this meant two chicks died before they left the nest, it was an excellent breeding record.

Life held many hazards for helpless young birds of prey, and parent birds were doing well if they raised one or two young a year. The high death rate among the young birds, both in the nest and during their first year on their own, was a harsh but effective way of keeping the species strong. Only the healthiest and best hunters survived to breed. The raising of three healthy young in their first breeding season together had been a remarkable feat for Artemis and Zeus.

Each year the two peregrines nested at the same cliff on the Palisades. Each year they chose the same ledge for their eyrie and raised one or more young, undisturbed by wild predators or humans. But the peace of their first few years together did not last.

In 1950 the cliff-top forests were disturbed. A road, the Palisades Parkway, was built along the west bank of the river. Workmen came to the cliffs with heavy, noisy machinery. Trees were cut down, and rocks blasted away.

The construction activity alarmed the nesting peregrines. Accustomed to peace and quiet, they were upset by the sounds of dynamite explosions and bulldozers. The delicate biological balances that produced the proper sequence of nesting behavior were disturbed. Some of the Palisades peregrines did not mate or make nesting scrapes in the gravel that year. Some falcons laid eggs but failed to incubate them.

That spring, for the first time, Zeus and Artemis did not raise a single young bird. That spring, not one young peregrine was raised on the Palisades.

The peregrine watchers on the Hudson's eastern bank hoped that the birds would nest again when the new road was finished. They counted heavily on the peregrines' attachment to their favorite nesting sites.

Most of the Palisades birds did try again to nest at their home ledges. But the new road had changed the Palisades forever. Now it was easy for people to visit the cliffs. They drove cars up and down the Palisades Parkway and picnicked on the cliff tops where they enjoyed spectacular views of the Hudson River below.

Most of the drivers and picnickers who used the Palisades Parkway meant no harm to the peregrines. In time, the nesting birds probably could have adjusted to the unfamiliar human activity. But the birds faced far more serious threats.

In 1951, Zeus and Artemis hatched two eggs. When the eyasses were four weeks old, a falconer waited on top of the cliff until the parents left the ledge to hunt. He climbed down the cliff and took one chick from the eyrie.

The second chick survived in the wild. But that chick was the last peregrine ever raised on the Palisades.

Year after year, Zeus and Artemis continued trying to nest at their cliff. Never again were they successful. Other peregrine pairs failed again and again too. When old birds died, there were no young birds to replace them.

Zeus the tiercel died in 1956. Artemis found no new mate. She returned alone to the nesting cliff each spring for five more years. Then she disappeared. Artemis was the last peregrine falcon ever seen by the bird watchers along the Hudson River.

The Hudson peregrine watchers hated to see the birds disappear. But they felt helpless. They blamed the new highway for the peregrines' troubles, and they couldn't remove the road. They hoped that in wilder places the birds were safe. The Hudson peregrine watchers were wrong. Their peregrines did not disappear because of the Palisades Parkway. The Hudson River birds died out for another reason—one that was affecting peregrines in wilder places too.

Nike, the large, golden daughter of Zeus and Artemis, had found a home and a mate in New England. In the spring of 1948, the young falcon and her mate nested on a cliff at the edge of a large lake in the Berkshire Hills of Massachusetts.

It was a perfect site for a peregrine eyrie, a place called by bird watchers an "ecological magnet." This meant that the site had qualities that drew peregrine pairs year after year. When a tiercel died or deserted the cliff, it was quickly claimed by another. It had been used almost continuously for close to a century.

On their perfect cliff Nike and her mate selected a nesting ledge and prepared for their young. Nike laid three eggs in her first clutch. The eggs broke before they could hatch. The birds nested again and the falcon laid four eggs. Three broke. The fourth hatched, but the chick was weak and sickly and soon died.

The next spring Nike and her mate returned to their cliff. She laid five eggs in two separate clutches. None hatched. The following year there was only one egg, which broke. And the next spring Nike and the tiercel returned together to their cliff but did not mate. Nike never raised a chick.

All over Massachusetts Nike's story was repeated. Year after year there were no young peregrines raised in any of the fourteen known eyries in the state.

From other parts of the United States and Canada, long-time peregrine observers began to report breeding failures in eyries they knew. Many eggs never hatched. Some birds, including the Sun-Life falcon, were seen eating their own eggs. Each year fewer peregrines were raised. Each year more eyries were abandoned.

Still, no one realized the full extent of the problem. Peregrine falcons had never been common birds. Many pairs had nested far away from towns, in wild areas where few people ever saw them. Even in a good year, only about two hundred chicks might have been raised in the entire eastern half of the United States. Peregrines lived as long as twenty years, so bird watchers continued to see adult falcons who had not raised chicks. And migrating peregrines who nested in Alaska and northern Canada continued to appear.

A few experts began to investigate peregrine nesting failures in their own areas. They studied eggs that failed to hatch and eggs that cracked. The eggshells were much thinner than they should have been and weighed 20 percent less than normal peregrine falcon eggshells.

It was not hard to see what was happening. Eggshells were too thin to support the weight of the incubating falcon, too thin to protect the growing embryos. Chicks died inside the eggs, or the eggs cracked and the partly developed embryos were eaten by the parents.

Figuring out *why* the eggshells were too thin was a little

more difficult. But there was one important clue. Peregrine falcons weren't the only birds that had suffered nesting failures. Other species with nesting problems had been studied and had seemed to be affected by pesticides like DDT.

Pesticides were sprayed on crops. The powerful chemicals were poisonous to insects that destroyed crops, but they were poisonous to other animals too. Small songbirds in a field at the time of a spraying died quickly. Others were poisoned when they ate insects or seeds from sprayed fields.

Pesticide settled into the soil, washed into rivers and streams, where it was taken into the tiny plants and animals that provided food for fish. When birds ate fish, they picked up pesticide. It was stored in their body fat and began to affect them in a number of harmful ways. Most important, DDT interfered with the birds' ability to secrete calcium carbonate, the main ingredient in eggshells. Without enough calcium carbonate, eggshells were weak. In some cases, birds contaminated by DDT laid eggs with no shells at all, just a thin membrane surrounding the embryo.

How could the peregrines, who did not eat fish, be harmed by DDT? Experts guessed that the peregrines were affected when they ate fish-eating and insect-eating birds. Also, they theorized, peregrines found it easy to catch birds that were crippled from eating pesticide.

The theory seemed to fit. Nesting failures among peregrine falcons had first been noticed soon after DDT came into widespread use in the late 1940s. As the inexpensive, easy-to-use pesticide grew more popular, the peregrine nesting failures spread. Unhatched eggs and dead peregrines were found to contain alarming amounts of pesticide.

All over the world the use of pesticides grew. In those places where DDT use was heaviest, peregrine falcons were disappearing rapidly. Even the Arctic-nesting birds might soon be affected by pesticide use in South America, where they wintered.

In 1965 peregrine falcon experts from many different countries held a conference and compared their findings. They discovered that peregrines were in trouble in many parts of the world, largely because of pesticides. Everywhere, they decided, the situation was critical. The peregrine falcon was an endangered species.

Nowhere was the peregrine more endangered than in the United States. In 1942, a group of people had taken a census of peregrines breeding east of the Rocky Mountains. They had found 275 active eyries—sites where pairs of birds were raising young. In 1964 a second census was taken. This time not one active eyrie was found.

The future for peregrine falcons in North America looked bleak. Most of the experts had no hope. Sadly they concluded that in the eastern United States the peregrine falcon was gone forever.

CHAPTER SEVEN

New Hope for the Peregrines

Thousands of miles to the north and west of the Hudson river area from which the falcons had disappeared was a breeding ground for Arctic peregrines. The Alaskan land above the Arctic Circle, north of the craggy mountains of the Brooks Range, was tundra, rolling and treeless. In winter the land lay frozen under many feet of snow, and few creatures tried to live there. During the short Arctic summer the land was transformed. The snow melted, and low-growing plants bloomed, covering the tundra with color for a few weeks.

Each year as winter ended, migrating peregrines returned to Alaska. There they nested and raised young. When the brief summer ended, the young birds and their parents migrated south. The effects of pesticides and pollution had not yet begun to show in the Arctic peregrines. This was probably because they ate DDT-contaminated prey only half the year, during the winter in South America. In the middle of the 1960s, when the falcons were gone from the eastern United States and fast disappearing from most of the west, the Alaskan birds were not yet in trouble.

In some parts of the Alaskan tundra peregrines nested right on the ground. But they preferred cliff eyries wherever they were available. This preference, combined with the birds' liking for water, made the cliffs along the Colville River a perfect place for peregrines.

In the summer of 1967 a pair of peregrines nested on a bare cliff along the Colville River as they had for several years. For the birds it was an ordinary breeding season. However, one of their chicks hatched that spring would prove to be very important to the whole species.

While the Colville River peregrines were nesting, a scientist at the Cornell University Laboratory of Ornithology in Ithaca, New York, was working on a plan. Dr. Tom Cade wanted to breed peregrine falcons in captivity. If it could be done, captive-bred birds might someday be set free on the wild cliffs where peregrines had once lived.

Most people believed that peregrines would not breed in captivity. No one could reproduce the conditions necessary for the birds' courtship flights, they said. They also pointed out that captive birds trained for falconry often seemed to regard their human owners as their mates and would have nothing to do with other peregrines.

Dr. Cade knew that the pessimists could be right. But he also thought he might overcome the problems. Perhaps birds who had never nested before, who had never even flown, could adjust to captivity. If they knew nothing of open spaces and towering cliffs, they wouldn't miss those things when they reached breeding age. If they were handled very rarely, they would prefer peregrine to human "mates."

Peregrine falcons had once nested in Ithaca. But now they were gone, as they were from all their old eyries nearby. The young peregrines for the breeding program would have to come from far away. Dr. Cade had studied the peregrines of the Alaskan tundra and knew of many eyries there. Although the peregrines were protected by law, he received special permission to take a few eyasses for Project Peregrine. His plan was to take only one eyass from each nest he visited, leaving the others to be raised by their parents.

The Colville River peregrines usually nested undisturbed. No roads led to their cliff, and the closest town was many miles away. The birds were not used to the sight of humans, so both the falcon and the tiercel were very upset when Dr. Cade approached their cliff. The falcon sat on the nesting ledge, protecting the eyasses. The tiercel flew and dived, screaming loudly, trying to scare the intruder away.

Dr. Cade climbed slowly toward the nesting ledge. The falcon, blocking his view of the eyasses, glared menacingly. Only when she realized that the man was not to be frightened away did she leave the ledge.

Both parent birds continued to threaten from the air as Dr. Cade looked over the eyasses. They were the right age—between three and four weeks old. Quickly he reached out and selected a strong-looking young falcon, already noticeably larger than her brothers. He put her inside his coat to protect her from the chill winds of the Arctic summer. The parent birds did not return to the ledge until he had left the cliff.

Back in Ithaca after a plane ride inside a dark box, the

young peregrine falcon from Alaska was placed in a big barn. There she had room to move around and had many different perches, but she could not escape. Within a short time she was named Cadey.

Cadey grew up and learned to fly inside the barn. She behaved like a normal peregrine, except that she didn't hunt for herself but was fed by humans. For a while she was flown by a falconer, and she proved to be an excellent hunter. But in order to keep her wild, to keep her from forming a strong attachment to a human, Cadey was not flown often.

Cadey was not the only falcon at Cornell. She was soon joined by other peregrines. Some, like Cadey, were taken from nests in Alaska. One of these Alaskan birds was a tiercel taken from a tundra eyrie at the age of three weeks. As he grew up, he had developed a playful, agreeable character. The tiercel had a habit of peering at people intently while turning his head until it was nearly upside-down. He looked very strange and not at all dignified in this position. The tiercel's comic habits earned him the name Heyoka, which is a Sioux Indian word for a clown, or someone who does everything backwards.

Other peregrines were donated to the breeding program by falconers who hoped that their birds could help to save the species. (There were other birds of prey too—golden eagles, goshawks, lanner falcons, prairie falcons.) The birds were kept in makeshift housing wherever room was available. The breeding program could not begin until a suitable place was found where birds of prey could feel comfortable and safe enough to nest.

Cornell University built a long barn that proved to be a perfect place for peregrine apartments. Each finished enclosure was two stories tall with big windows on the outside wall to let in the sunlight. The opposite wall had small windows with one-way glass so human observers could watch the birds without disturbing them. The two side walls had several gravel-covered wooden ledges at different heights from the floor, so the birds could choose their own nesting, feeding, and sleeping ledges as they would in the wild.

By 1971, the bird barn was ready. Would the birds like their new apartments? Would they accept the mates humans chose for them? Would they breed in these strange surroundings?

Heyoka was placed in an apartment with an older falcon named Lydia. Lydia had been captured by a falconer during her first migration and trained for hunting. It was hoped that in time she would feel more comfortable with another peregrine than she did with humans.

Project Peregrine had enough birds to make up three

more pairs, with one falcon left over—Cadey. In the beginning, she would have no mate, but she seemed happy enough alone.

In fact, none of the peregrines seemed to appreciate company, at least not at first. The birds apparently preferred being alone. By the time some of them showed signs of accepting their mates, summer had ended and the breeding season was over.

The four pairs of peregrines remained together during the fall and winter. The following spring, two pairs courted and mated. The falcons began to lay eggs. Heyoka tried to court Lydia, but every time he approached, she chased him away.

Meanwhile, the first clutches of eggs were taken away from the two mated pairs of peregrines. When eggs are destroyed or stolen, wild birds often lay a second clutch, as Nike had done when her eggs broke. The Project Peregrine people hoped to hatch the first clutches in incubators while the birds produced more eggs. But all the first eggs were infertile.

The two falcons laid more eggs, and one of the second clutches was fertile. The eggs were carefully placed in incubators normally used to hatch chicken eggs and kept at a constant high temperature and humidity. Unfortunately, the temperature and humidity that were right for hatching

chickens turned out to be wrong for hatching falcons. The incubators were too hot and too moist. The peregrine embryos died inside the shells.

By late summer it was clear that there would be no young peregrines that year. It also seemed clear that Lydia would never accept a peregrine mate. She was removed from Heyoka's apartment and Cadey took her place.

At first, Cadey didn't like living with Heyoka any better than Lydia had. She complained constantly, as if her only wish were to be rid of the troublesome tiercel. She was ready to fight whenever Heyoka came near. But Heyoka persisted, courting her and offering food, and in a few weeks they were sharing meals and behaving like a mated pair.

Another long winter passed. In March 1973 the four pairs of peregrines in the bird barn began their normal spring courtship ritual. Heyoka called to Cadey, inviting her to share his meals of chicken and quail, showing her possible nesting ledges. The birds billed and preened each other and shared a sleeping ledge. Their apartment allowed no room for aerial acrobatics, but the great flight displays were not necessary. The birds began to mate, and on April 12, Cadey laid an egg.

Within a week the clutch of four eggs was complete, and Cadey began to incubate. On April 27 the eggs were removed. Dr. Cade had discovered by observing other birds of prey living in the bird barn that leaving the eggs with the parents for one week of incubation improved their chances of hatching normally. If the eggs were left longer, the parents were unlikely to produce another clutch.

Cadey fussed and shrieked when her eggs were taken. She even struck at the human hand reaching into the nest. But she soon settled down again, and within two weeks she produced the first egg of a second clutch. When the four eggs from the second clutch were removed, the falcon remained calm. Cadey and Heyoka produced one more clutch of four eggs that spring.

Cadey's entire first clutch was fertile. The precious eggs were placed in an incubator. Temperature and humidity were checked several times each day. The eggs would not be overheated again. Neither would they be allowed to become too cold or too dry. There was nothing left to do but wait.

For three weeks the eggs sat silently in the incubator. Then, faint noises could be heard. The peregrines were almost ready to hatch.

Inside the first egg, a tiny peregrine lay curled up with its head tucked under a stubby wing. Running from the top of its head to the middle of its neck was a large muscle called the hatching muscle. Thirty days after the start of incubation, a sudden contraction of the hatching muscle snapped the peregrine's head back from its position under the wing. The bird's egg tooth hit the inside of the eggshell, forming a pip—a small hole with thin cracks radiating from it.

Everyone working for Project Peregrine knew that once the egg was pipped, it would soon hatch. But no one knew for sure just how soon. One person guessed ten hours. Someone else said twenty-four. A third person said maybe forty hours.

After forty hours nothing had happened. The baby continued to make noises inside the egg, so it was still alive. But for how long? Maybe the little bird was in trouble and needed help getting out of the egg. In the wild, mother birds sometimes help their young. This bird might die of exhaustion in its struggle to be hatched.

On the other hand, maybe there was nothing wrong at all. Maybe some peregrines took a long time between pipping and hatching. If the bird were not ready to hatch, the blood vessels attaching it to the food supply in the egg would still be functioning. Breaking the egg then might cause the peregrine to bleed to death in a few seconds.

It was decided to leave the egg alone. Anxiously, the Project Peregrine people waited as hour after hour dragged by. Finally, fifty-five hours after pipping, the egg began to shake as the baby moved vigorously inside.

Soon, a crack appeared in the shell. The little peregrine pushed itself around inside the egg, sawing a neat line with its egg tooth. In ten minutes of sawing, then resting, then *cheep*ing, then sawing some more, the bird made a perfect ring in the shell, splitting it in two pieces.

After a minute's rest, the peregrine gave a great push, and half the eggshell fell away. But it wasn't hatched yet. The tiny bird was still confined by the other half of the eggshell. After another short rest and some more complaining, the peregrine wriggled around so that its feet rested on the edge of the shell.

With one last burst of energy, the bird pushed down with its feet and fell out of the shell, flat on its belly. Wet and scrawny, and too exhausted from its struggle even to *cheep,* the bird lay still. Project Peregrine's first falcon was born.

CHAPTER EIGHT

Return of the Peregrines

The dramatic scene in the bird barn's hatching room was repeated many times that summer. Three of the four peregrine pairs produced fertile eggs, and twenty-two babies were hatched in the incubator.

The baby peregrines demanded constant attention, and the humans who cared for them soon found themselves as busy as tiercels and falcons. Perhaps they were even busier because in addition to acting as foster parents, they were scientists trying to learn as much as possible about their charges.

Shortly after hatching, each little peregrine was checked to make sure it was healthy and then weighed. Most of the newly hatched birds weighed about thirty-five grams, not much more than one ounce. The eggshell was weighed also, to determine whether the captive birds had pesticides in their systems. Most of the eggshells were just a bit lighter than they should have been—even the grain fed to the chickens and quail that were raised for peregrine food must have contained traces of pesticides.

After weighing, a newly hatched bird was returned to the incubator to rest for a few hours. Under the warm light, the peregrine's white down dried in little clumps. If the baby had dried under a falcon's body, her feathers would have fluffed the down naturally. With a baby hatched in the incubator, down-fluffing became a task for a human foster parent. And the best tool for this operation proved to be a soft toothbrush.

Next, each baby's head was marked with a different color felt-tip marker. This way, observers could tell the babies apart and keep accurate records on each one. In a few weeks, when the colored down was replaced by feathers, each bird would receive a leg band with an identifying number.

A newly hatched peregrine needed food more than anything else. But the baby birds didn't seem to know that. The first feeding of Cadey's chick was typical of many first meals that followed. It began when a human foster parent placed the baby on a soft towel. Then he picked up a bit of quail meat in a tweezers and held it in front of the little bird. The peregrine did nothing. It lay sprawled on the towel, unable to sit up or even lift its head.

The bird would need coaxing to open its mouth. The human called to the peregrine, *chup, chup, p-chup*. This was the noise a falcon used when feeding her young, and although the baby bird had never heard its mother, it understood the cry. The chick struggled to sit up. Its mouth opened wide. But before the food could be thrust into its beak, the little peregrine lost its precarious balance and fell over.

The bird seemed discouraged. *P-chup*, called the human. Again the chick sat up, but once again it promptly fell over. On the third try the human decided that the peregrine needed more help. This time when the bird sat up, he supported it gently with the fingers of one hand. In the other hand he held the tweezers full of quail meat.

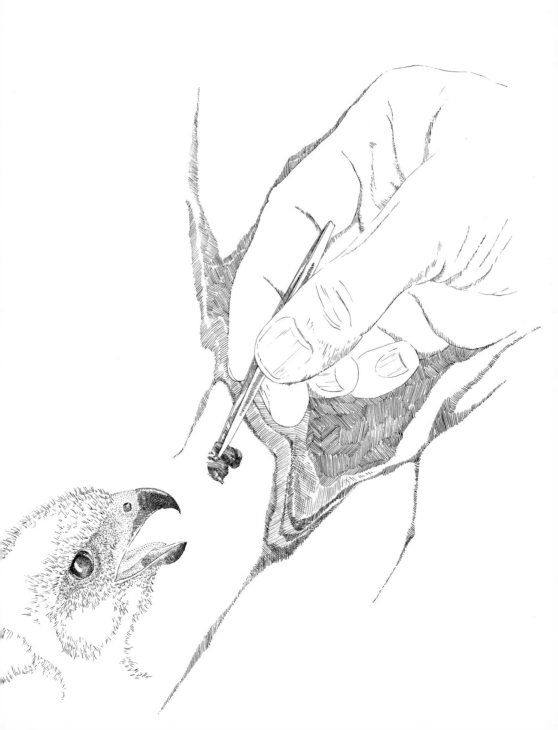

Chup, chup, he called again. The bird opened its mouth and in went the food. Baby peregrines seem to wear a permanently surprised expression, but this bird looked more surprised than usual as it swallowed the quail meat. Suddenly it seemed to understand the whole peculiar business with the man and the tweezers. By the second mouthful, the peregrine was an eating expert.

The feeding ended after only a few bites. The peregrine would have been happy to eat more, but too much food at one time could have made it sick or even have killed it. Instead of one or two big meals a day, the little peregrine needed a small meal every two hours.

With each meal the peregrine grew more eager to eat. It soon needed little coaxing. It opened its mouth and cried even before it saw the food. Soon it began to reach out for the meat, stretching its neck and flapping its stubby wings to keep from falling over. In this way, the bird was developing the muscles it would need to fly.

The peregrine grew so fast that sometimes its human foster parents imagined it growing before their eyes. When it was six days old, it had doubled its birth weight. At three weeks of age, the eyass was ten times its size at hatching.

Some of the peregrines were cared for by humans until they were able to care for themselves in their own apartments in the bird barn. But most of the eyasses were returned to their peregrine parents when they were between two and three weeks old. By then, the parents had finished producing eggs for the season and so could care for their young.

The four babies from Cadey and Heyoka's first clutch were the first to be introduced to their parents. No one was sure that the falcon and the tiercel would accept their young and care for them properly. The eyasses were slipped in through a trap door and set down on the nesting ledge. Several pairs of human eyes watched anxiously through the one-way glass. The people were prepared to rescue the babies if Cadey or Heyoka attacked.

They need not have worried. Cadey adopted her babies immediately, behaving as if she had hatched and reared them without human interference. She was a perfect falcon mother. Heyoka took longer to adjust to his fatherly role. At first he seemed confused, and he ignored the eyasses. It didn't really matter since the peregrines were fed regularly, and he was not needed to hunt. But within a few days, he seemed to realize what had happened and began to behave like a normal peregrine father.

With the excellent care they received from their human foster parents and their real peregrine parents, twenty of the twenty-two eyasses survived and learned to fly in the bird barn. In the wild, three fertile pairs of falcons probably would not have produced more than six or seven young who survived to become independent.

The 1974 breeding season was even more successful. Once again Cadey and Heyoka produced three clutches of eggs and were perfect parents for the eyasses they raised. That season, five peregrine pairs produced twenty-three young. Everyone began to look forward to the time when the birds who were hatched during the first year would be old enough for breeding.

Some people had claimed that falcons hatched in captivity would never be completely normal; that is, they would never breed. These pessimists were proved wrong in 1974, when a pair of Cornell-bred prairie falcons, a species closely related to peregrines, mated and produced fertile eggs. Their young grew up healthy and normal.

The Cornell project had proved that it was possible to breed peregrines in captivity. It had proved that captive-born falcons would grow up to breed normally. There was only one thing left to prove—that peregrines born and raised in captivity could survive in the wild. Only if some of the Cornell birds were released, learned to depend on themselves, established eyries, and produced young could Dr.

Cade achieve his goal—to save the peregrines from extinction and return them to their original territories in the United States, where DDT was now banned. He believed that if the DDT ban were strictly enforced, peregrine falcons would thrive again.

Again there were pessimists who said it would never be possible to release the peregrines born in the bird barn. Even in an area where pesticides were no longer in use, the birds would never survive. They were too tame, too used to being fed by humans. And didn't peregrines learn to hunt by watching their parents? Would a bird bred in captivity know what to do when it saw a pigeon?

These questions were answered by accident, much sooner than anyone expected. One young tiercel born in captivity had been flown by a falconer but had never been taught to kill live prey. Throughout the fall and winter seasons the tiercel was flown. All the while he was fed by humans. Suddenly one day in early spring, he noticed the small birds that were his natural prey. He began to stoop at pigeons and starlings, and in a short time started to catch them. Clearly, he had learned to hunt entirely on his own. Soon after this, the tiercel began to chase and attack other birds of prey who entered his hunting territory. Finally, one day he failed to return home after chasing an intruder. The tiercel was not seen again in Ithaca, but the Project Peregrine people hoped he had reached the foggy Canadian coast and there found a mate.

Although this tiercel's experience was a good sign, Dr. Cade did not want to release a lot of young, inexperienced peregrines and hope for the best. Without help, many or most of the birds would die before they learned to hunt. What the peregrines needed was a sort of halfway station between captivity and independence in the wild.

A halfway station could be a man-made, protected eyrie near a natural cliff where peregrines had once lived. The birds would be placed in the eyrie when they were four weeks old, about a week before they were ready to fly. A human foster parent would continue to care for them, feeding them even after they were flying. The young peregrines would quickly begin to hunt on their own. When they could catch their own prey, their foster parent would stop feeding them.

The Project Peregrine people hoped that the birds they released would not migrate. Migration meant the birds would pass through unprotected areas, where ignorant people might shoot them, or where powerful pesticides were still in use. They hoped that the birds would find everything they needed at the safe cliffs where they were released and remain there to breed.

At the end of the 1974 breeding season, four young peregrines were released to a halfway station. Their parents were
Cadey and Heyoka. If all went well, Cadey's grandchildren
would be wild peregrines. Through human interference the
peregrines had almost disappeared. With human help perhaps they would be saved.

BIBLIOGRAPHICAL NOTE

My research on peregrine falcons began with *Grzimek's Animal Life Encyclopedia, Volume 7/Birds I* (New York: Van Nostrand Reinhold Company, 1972). This book provided me with essential background on the biology and habits of birds of prey. The papers given at the 1965 conference on peregrines were collected in a book edited by Joseph J. Hickey, *Peregrine Falcon Populations: Their Biology and Decline* (Madison: University of Wisconsin Press, 1969). I found two of these papers particularly useful— Joseph A. Hagar's study of Massachusetts peregrines and an account by Richard A. Herbert and Kathleen Green Skelton Herbert of the disappearance of the Hudson River peregrines.

I then discovered that while there were many books on falconry, there were few on wild peregrine behavior. And most of these accounts proved sketchy or misleading. Therefore I turned to the Project Peregrine people at Cornell University for information on wild birds as well as the captive peregrines in their breeding program. Dr. Tom Cade, who directs the project, sent me his written materials and allowed me to visit the bird barn. Jim Weaver, who runs the bird barn, shared with me his knowledge and appreciation of the falcons. He also arranged for me to be in the barn at the right time to see a hatching; without doubt, this was the high point of my research. Both men carefully read my manuscript and made many excellent suggestions. It was their interest and help that made *The Peregrine Falcons* possible.

ABOUT THE AUTHOR

Alice Schick grew up on Long Island. After graduating from Northwestern University in Chicago, she returned to New York to become a textbook editor and a free-lance writer. Her first book, *Kongo and Kumba: Two Gorillas,* was a Junior Literary Guild selection.

Ms. Schick is active in a number of animal-oriented organizations. In researching *The Peregrine Falcons* she observed the experimental project at Cornell that is attempting to breed peregrines and reestablish them in the wild.

She and her husband, Joel, and their six cats live in Massachusetts.

ABOUT THE ARTIST

As a child, Peter Parnall lived for some time in the desert. There he developed the strong interest in birds and animals that has characterized his illustrating career.

Mr. Parnall has illustrated over three dozen books, several of which have appeared on *The New York Times* Best Illustrated list. His striking drawings of birds frequently appear in *Audubon* Magazine.